TOP DOGS

PORTRAITS AND STORIES

DIANE COSTELLO

AMHERST MEDIA, INC.   BUFFALO, NY

ABOUT THE AUTHOR

Diane Costello, owner of Fog Dog Studios, is an award-winning pet portrait photographer based in Half Moon Bay, CA. She holds her Master of Photography degree and is a Professional Photographers of America Certified Professional Photographer. Diane has been involved in photography for over 20 years and is always working toward perfecting her artistic vision and sharing her knowledge with others.

Copyright © 2018 by Diane Costello.
All rights reserved.
All photographs by the author unless otherwise noted.

Published by:
Amherst Media, Inc.
PO BOX 538
Buffalo, NY 14213
www.AmherstMedia.com

Publisher: Craig Alesse
Senior Editor/Production Manager: Michelle Perkins
Editors: Barbara A. Lynch-Johnt, Beth Alesse
Acquisitions Editor: Harvey Goldstein
Associate Publisher: Katie Kiss
Editorial Assistance from: Carey A. Miller, Roy Bakos, Jen Sexton-Riley, Rebecca Rudell
Business Manager: Sarah Loder
Marketing Associate: Tonya Flickinger

ISBN-13: 978-1-68203-320-3
Library of Congress Control Number: 2017948040
Printed in the United States of America
10 9 8 7 6 5 4 3 2 1

AUTHOR A BOOK WITH AMHERST MEDIA!

Are you an accomplished photographer with devoted fans? Consider authoring a book with us and share your quality images and wisdom with your fans. It's a great way to build your business and brand through a high-quality, full-color printed book sold worldwide. Our experienced team makes it easy and rewarding for each book sold—no cost to you. E-mail **submissions@amherstmedia.com** *today!*

www.facebook.com/AmherstMediaInc
www.youtube.com/AmherstMedia
www.twitter.com/AmherstMedia

CONTENTS

INTRODUCTION

Every dog has a story and every dog lucky enough to find their forever home has a human who has a story. Some of our stories will be similar and some drastically different, but that is what makes them all so amazing. I am a firm believer that your dog finds you—even when you have no idea they are supposed to be a part of your life.

For years, I had a day job that didn't make me happy; it simply was not fulfilling. One day, I guess I'd had enough. I could not handle the commute any longer. I no longer felt I could handle a job that I was not emotionally invested in. Perhaps it was the loss of my family's dog, a 14-year-old Rottie named Bear, followed a few months later by the loss of my dad, that helped to

push me to my limit. It was all too much, and I just couldn't do it anymore—so I quit.

I had to ask myself what was next. I took on a contract job in the pet care industry. It was something completely different and out of the ordinary for me. It was exhilarating, and I felt free. I was besieged by dog kisses and wiggles and snuggles and full of slobber—and I got more exercise than I knew what to do with. I loved hanging out with the dogs and getting to know every single one. I had always loved photography but had concentrated on landscapes and portraits. I started carrying my camera to work and photographing the dogs playing, sitting, lying, jumping, running, and sleeping. About halfway through my first year caring for other people's pets, my husband decided our house had been too quiet and it was time for us to get a dog. He informed me that he had found a Boxer pup who would be ready to come home right after Christmas. I was great with it. This puppy, whom we named Gromit, turned my world upside-down, from the minute we brought him home to the day we had to say goodbye. In his short 7 years, he taught me patience. He showed me how to not be a pushover and when to use my big voice. He taught me how to read dogs' body language and see the subtle changes—even though his 100 different looks, at first, seemed the same. He also taught me how to train him.

Gromit came into my life when I didn't know I needed him. He left my life when I needed him even more. Gromit passed from lung cancer just 10 days after he was diagnosed. He had just turned 7 years old. My

life was shattered. My heart was broken into millions of pieces, and I had no idea how to pick them up and keep going. Gromit helped me build my pet portrait business and to make it what it is today. He was my heart.

You'll read more about Gromit—and the pup named Dot whom my husband and I later adopted—in the following section of the book. You'll also read stories about other dog adoptions, fun stories about dog antics, and the many ways dogs touch our hearts and fill our lives with love.

A FOREVER HOME

HEART DOG

This is Gromit, the Boxer puppy who really started the ball rolling toward my business in fine art pet portraiture. He was the love of my life. In this image, he is just 3 months of age—and absolutely adorable!

Gromit was my husband's idea/pick/project, which soon became mine. He did all the looking and searching and eventually found Gromit through an ad. He was listed as AKC registered, with papers and all. We didn't think anything of it nor did we know any better. Knowing he was AKC registered meant the breeder knew what she was doing, right? We didn't know that, although the breeder meant well, she was a backyard breeder who didn't really test or breed for health. She was not a puppy mill owner; she only had the one litter from Gromit's momma, and she adored and cared for those pups. She loved that we kept in touch with her and that we absolutely loved our Gromit. He was the cutest little thing with a little black teddy bear silhouette on his nose (which eventually became a black blob). Gromit was bouncy and happy and silly and goofy and zoomie. He was not what most people think of when they think of a Boxer. He was not a jumpy overzealous Boxer; he was a watcher—and a smart little guy, too.

We brought Gromit home just a few days after Christmas. We still had our holiday decorations up, which included bells hanging around our front door. Gromit learned that if he rang those bells, the front door would open—magically. He only had two accidents in the house because of that. He also would just go over and start ringing those bells just because he wanted to go outside and play.

Gromit came with a number of health problems that started to rear their ugly heads as he grew up. He had many bouts of tummy troubles and pancreatitis. He was diagnosed with Boxer cardiomyopathy (ARVC) when he was 3. He had a mass cell tumor removed from his side around the age of 4. He was allergic to chicken. Gromit inhaled a foxtail and was rushed to the vet to have it removed. Two weeks later, he inhaled another foxtail—this time, it was in the other nostril. Again, we rushed him to the vet to have it removed. Gromit scratched one eye and then, a couple of months later, scratched the other. It was never a dull moment, and our vet knew us very well.

Gromit grew into an 85-pound lap dog. He was known throughout the community as the most well-behaved Boxer people had ever seen. As he grew older, he had issues with his back. The discs were fusing on the top of his vertebrae, making it more difficult for him to move around.

Despite all his issues, Gromit was a very distinguished and regal, gentle dog. It was lung cancer that took him from us at the young age of 7. He will forever be missed!

DOT

After Gromit passed, I doubted I could ever own a dog again. But then I thought, "I am a portrait photographer who specializes in dogs. How can I not have another dog? Another Boxer?" Little did I know the deck was stacked against me. One day shy of 2 months after Gromit passed, a litter of rescue pups was born. I was asked if I might want to adopt one, but I didn't feel ready. I photographed the pups when they were almost 7 weeks old, to help get them adopted. Most of them were spoken for at the time I took the photos. A few weeks later, someone at the rescue asked if I was 100 percent positive I didn't want a pup. I answered, "No, I am *not* positive that I do not want a dog." And so, I brought home the pup who had caught my eye from the very beginning. She was tiny—just 5 pounds—and a snuggle bug. As I was lying in bed with this 9-week-old puppy snuggled up next to me, I began to sob. I apologized to Gromit—for I don't know what. All of a sudden, I smelled buttered popcorn. I realized that my husband was not home and all the windows were closed. Gromit was sending me a sign. His paws had smelled like buttered popcorn. He was telling me this little nugget of a puppy was meant to be with us. We welcomed the pup home and named her Dot.

FROM THE TRACK TO HOME

Tallulah has an amazing story in that she was a racing rescue. Left ear tattoo = 50868 (National Greyhound Association registration number). Right ear tattoo = 59A (birth date and order). Track name = Sweet Bee Cat. Life on the track is over for Tallulah.

Tallulah was adopted from Golden State Greyhound Adoption in 2014 and has since been living "the life" in the California coastal town of El Granada. She shares her home with two cats and her human momma, Libby. When she raced, Tallulah spent roughly 20 hours a day in a cage. Now she has free access to the backyard, four dog beds, two couches, and Libby's bed to choose from when she wants to snooze. Tallulah has walks on the beach, in the open space preserve, or around the neighborhood. She has a dog-walker twice a week, trips to visit her pal Pooch, and rides in the car pretty much always. She collects shoes and brings them to her bed—not to chew on, just to surround herself with. If there are no shoes available, she'll go for jackets, underwear, or messenger bags. That's just what Tallulah does, because Tallulah is a Greyhound and Greyhounds are just . . . well, Greyhounds!

Greyhounds like to lean against people or against each other. They "roo"—it's a form of singing unique to this breed. Greyhounds "roach," too; this is a pose they strike when they lie on their backs with their legs extended straight up. Also, Greyhounds have a tendency to "derp"; this is charac-

terized by a lolling of the tongue, between the teeth, out of the mouth. None of these activities is particularly elegant or graceful, yet Greyhounds are highly amusing and certainly endearing!

People often think they can't adopt a Greyhound because the dogs will need to

run 10 miles a day. This is simply not true. Some do like to run with their people, but most prefer a nap on the couch. Some folks feel they can't adopt a Greyhound because they live in an apartment. This isn't the case, either. Greyhounds are happy to nap on the couch most of the day, and they don't need a lot of room to do that. It's true that they need a good daily walk, but so do all other breeds!

So, is Tallulah spoiled? *Yes.* But anyone who meets one of these magical creatures is sure to spoil them. They are gentle spirits with soulful eyes and hearts as big as their muscles. They're goofy, graceful, rambunctious couch potatoes. They can be skittish and neurotic—or nonplussed over anything they encounter. One thing Greyhounds can count on is that they will always be loved, loving, and devoted. Tallulah certainly is!

KATELYN AND NACHO

Katelyn started volunteering at Muttville in November of 2015. She wanted to be involved with an amazing organization that rescues and re-homes senior dogs. She knew, one day, there was a chance that she just might bring one of the lovable seniors home.

Nacho, then known as Grover, was in one of the private areas because he wasn't fond of other dogs and preferred his own space. Katelyn realized because the dog was snappy, he might not have a great chance of finding a forever home. However, Katelyn had grown up with dogs who had challenging behaviors, and her parents had taught her patience goes a long way. She was ready to put in the effort required to help the dog adapt.

Realizing Grover was an outcast, Katelyn started paying special attention to him. During their first walk together, Grover stopped and looked up at Katelyn with his big, beautiful eyes and precious underbite.

She said she felt as if he was telling her, "Lady, I trust you. Please pick me up and carry me back to my bed." When she picked him up and held him in her arms, she did not want to let go. She told one of the Muttville employees she was interested in adopting Grover, filled out the paperwork, and by the following week, took the dog home. She said she was originally going to name him Thor, but when her Dad met him, he said, "He looks more like a Nacho." He was right, and Nacho it was.

Nacho settled in nicely with only a couple of minor scuffles with the family cats. After just a few months, he learned to share the love, and now everyone gets along great. Nacho is so special to Katelyn, and she is thankful for organizations like Muttville that give older dogs a second chance to have a fur-ever home and a happy life.

Nacho, then known as Grover, was in one of the private areas because he wasn't fond of other dogs and preferred his own space.

ANGELS

Riley (Boxer), Molly (Shepherd mix) and Oliver each have their own story on how they became part of this amazing pack. Riley (formerly Joe Boxer) was adopted from a private shelter in Berkeley in 2005 at the age of 6 months. He was energetic, goofy, loving, and always happy. It was love at first sight for his new mom, Nancy. Riley was also a perfect fit for Nancy's husband Peter and their Cattle Dog mix, Gus.

Nancy had always wanted to train a therapy dog, and Riley had the perfect personality for the job. After all of the obedience and therapy classes—a long, time-consuming process—Riley graduated from the program at the age of 2. He had two long-term assignments, one with the residents of an adult care facility and the other with a local library participating in the Paws to Tales program, which helps children become more confident readers by reading aloud to specially trained dogs. Riley, now 12, retired from his therapy work in May of 2017.

Molly (the Unsinkable Molly Brown) was originally adopted by Nancy's neighbor, who had never had a dog before. Molly was kept in her yard all day, howling and crying. Nancy and Riley would visit Molly. Molly's owner decided Molly really needed to go to a home that would give her the attention and love she craved. Nancy stepped in to help Molly find a new home. In the process, she would walk Molly, bringing her over to her home to hang out with her gang. During this time, Nancy's husband Peter fell in love with Molly and suggested they keep her. She became a part of the pack and is definitely a daddy's girl.

Gus, a dog that had been part of Nancy and Peter's family earlier, had crossed the rainbow bridge years before and with Riley and Molly getting older, Nancy decided it was time to bring another dog into their home. Oliver (formerly Pony), a young Beagle/Jack Russell Terrier mix, was adopted from the San Francisco Humane Society. He is feisty, insecure, and a bit skittish, so Oliver has been a work in progress. He is the pack's special boy, the one who needs a little more reassurance and patience.

Riley (Boxer), Molly (Shepherd mix) and Oliver each have their own story on how they became part of this amazing pack.

YOU SAVED ME

There's nothing like the bond shared between a person and their dog. This adoption story will reaffirm the importance of cherishing every moment you have with your pet.

"Let me tell you a story about little Shelby Roo," says Alana Kulper. "That dog was the first dog to truly change my life, inside and out. You see that picture of me with that sweet face in my hands? That right there, a moment captured by Diane Costello, embodies our entire relationship. This picture also happens to document the last moments we shared together in this life. I knew it, Shelby Roo knew it, and Diane knew it. It was by no means an easy night, but in that picture I was in the middle of telling her the story of how she came to find me.

'Roo, I don't know much about the beginning of your life. I do know that you were previously owned by some hotshot lawyers who would board you every summer while they went and traveled. Then it came time for them to grow their family into more than just the three of you, and just like that, three became four. An indoor dog quickly became and outdoor dog. I'm sure that you forgave them every time that they came out to give you attention, but that you were quickly disappointed whenever they went back inside without you.

'Boarding soon went from only two months in the summer to three or four months out of the year. You were aging gracefully, and your black face soon became dotted with gray hair. At your place of boarding, 7 years into your life, the universe decided that it was time for us to finally meet. I had seen you a few times, but you just blended into the crowd of all of the other dogs that boarded there, too. I was

told that they had finally left you there for good, that you would no longer be a part of their family. But that was okay, you would quickly become *my* family. I remember taking you out on a walk—just the two of us—to see if we could bond, and I snuck you home and took a nap with you. It was then that our fate was sealed. You were mine, I was yours, we just belonged to each other. Every time I came to the house to bring home the daycare dogs, you would jump at the gate, hoping I would take you; you cried with hope and looked defeated when I walked away without you. It wasn't long though, before you were able to be with me for the rest of your life.

'You saved me. When I suddenly parted ways with the facility that you were trapped in most of your life, I was lost. I didn't know which direction to go in, but you were there with your soft coat to soak up my tears. Remember when we used to walk 5 miles everyday with Auntie Diane and Grom? Rain or shine, you were up to the challenge of helping me through my tough times. It is partly because of you that I decided that it was time to step up and open my own dog-walking business. No matter what happened, you would be by my side, so how could that be bad? So we started our adventure into the unknown together; you took that leap with me, and we have been so successful. Thank you for helping me to weed out the dogs that truly aren't good with other dogs, and for always being so honest. You are my best friend, my partner in crime, the perfect shotgun rider (well, okay, not *shotgun* because you insisted on being on patrol in the back of the truck).

You have been the best bossy sidekick a girl could ask for. We will meet again someday, but thank you for giving me your last 5 years on this planet.'

"That night, I held my best friend's paw and told her we would meet again, that she was perfect, and that it was okay to go and no longer be in pain.

Shelby Roo taught me what it meant to truly, madly, deeply feel connected to an animal and to open myself up to the greatest love and greatest loss I have ever felt in this life. She rescued me; it was not the other way around."

TRIXIE

Trixie, an off-the-track rescued Greyhound, had only been in her new home for a few weeks when I was contacted to photographer her. She was just beginning to learn how to be a dog and a family member. It was so amazing to witness her playing/working her ball stuffed with treats. She had no idea what to do at first, but her nose kept telling her good stuff was just inside.

RANGER

Ranger has a wonderful adoption story. After a successful mother-daughter day of shopping, Sarah and her mom decided to stop by the newly renovated Peninsula Humane Society location. They wanted to check out the new facility but had no intention to adopt. They wandered through the new building and admired the indoor play yard and the quiet cat condos. Next, they started down the hallway to the dog wing and stopped in front of each room to read the dogs' profiles and talk to each and every pocket-sized dog. Suddenly, they found themselves standing in front of a room in which they saw a black dog curled tightly on an oversized chair. They couldn't tell what type of dog it was—or whether it was a boy or girl. It was hard to get a read on the tightly-curled dog in from of them.

The dog, whom the shelter had named Star, was a found stray from Pacifica. He was labeled as a Lab/Border Collie mix and described as timid but playful. He didn't move except to lift his head and stare. Sarah's mom looked at her and suggested they go in and meet the pup. They entered the room with the staff attendant. Star watched, still not moving from his curled position. Sarah's mom sat on the only folding chair in the room, and the attendant stood in the corner, so Sarah sat on the floor. Star raised himself up, giving the women a chance to see how big he was and to admire his tuxedo markings. He walked over to Sarah, sniffed her hand, and went straight to her lap where he preceded to curl up. He placed his head on her chest and let out a sigh. Sarah's mom whispered "That's *your* dog!" Sarah said she felt as if he picked her. Fighting the feeling of love at first sight, she looked for anything that might make the dog non-adoptable. She wasn't looking for a dog. Her rational mind took over, and she told her mom, "I can't have a dog with my schedule and lack of a yard." Her mom pleaded with her, saying she would help watch him when Sarah was at work. "Look at him look at you!" she exclaimed. She played with him a bit more before asking the attendant for a few minutes to talk. Sarah's mom repeated that she would help out on the days Sarah worked. Sarah had to stop and remind her mom that she did not live alone and needed to run the idea by her husband. Her mom agreed. Sarah called the house, spoke with her husband, Rick, and began to explain that she and her mom were at the shelter and found a dog, but before she could finish, Rick said "No!" Sarah tried repeatedly to explain the connection, but each time she did, her husband gave the same response.

Sarah and her mom talked to the staff and explained that they had to go home and get family approval before adoption. They drove 30 minutes to Sarah's house, strategizing the whole way. They explained to Rick that once he met Star, he would fall in love, too. They convinced him to ride back to the shelter to meet the pup and hoped

he would still be there. The group crammed into the room again, and Rick began to see how gentle the big black dog was. It seemed like forever before he finally agreed to the adoption. The couple completed the paperwork, and took the dog to his forever home. That night, as a family, they agreed that Star was not his name—they decided to call him Ranger.

PERSONALITY PLUS

GOURMET

Many dogs are food-driven. It can take a lot of training to teach a dog to wait before digging into a scrumptious treat.

Did you know that dogs will suck in spaghetti just like kids and some adults? I had no idea this was even possible. I could not do this with just any dog, because the spaghetti with marinara sauce would have probably disappeared in one swift gulp. Gromit would not touch it unless he was given the okay, which made working with him on different food projects easy. I gave him one noodle, no sauce, to see what he would do. I was fascinated when he tried to eat it and then started sucking it up.

A DARLING DIVA

Isn't she sweet? This is my pup, Dot, at just 10 weeks old. Even at this young age, she was a pro at posing. She's a real diva, and I chose to photograph her against a white backdrop to ensure that all of the focus would be on her.

Dot loves to climb up her daddy, perch on the top of his recliner, and stare down at him (like Snoopy on his doghouse in the *Charlie Brown* comics and cartoons). If Dot doesn't think you are getting out of bed fast enough to feed her, she will sit on your chest and stare at you until you open your eyes. She tends to get jumpy and, even though she is a mere 11 pounds, it's a bit uncomfortable. Dottie curls up on her blanket when she sleeps next to me but climbs under the blankets to sleep next to her daddy.

Dot loves people and other dogs—big dogs, little dogs, it just doesn't matter, she loves to play with them. She also *loves* her clothes! Yes, she has a number of cute little jackets. She gets cold often and likes to wear her coats. Despite her girlishness, she is part tomboy and plays really rough with her siblings. She has earned a host of nicknames, including Gremlin, Tazmanian Devil, Lunatic, and Spaz, to name a few. She loves to be the center of attention but has the attention span of a gnat. Everyone who meets Dot falls in love with her.

THEIR HOLIDAY BEST

Though it may seem like a good idea to give a puppy or adult dog as a holiday gift, it is not. A dog is a big commitment, and adoption should be carefully planned for. Also, the holidays are hectic, and bringing a new pet into the home will likely compound the stress. Finally, in winter, the weather is often horrible, and this can make housetraining more difficult.

If you have a dog, remember to keep holiday sweets out of his or her reach. Both chocolate and Xylitol (found in certain gums, candies, toothpaste and baked goods) can be lethal to dogs.

BELOVED BABIES

This 4-month-old Boston Terrier *(below)* was a bundle of energy when I photographed him. There was no way to keep him standing or sitting still on the floor of my studio—without taping him down, and I wasn't going to do *that!*

I placed him on my white barrel chair to improve the odds of getting a great portrait. There's something about the lure of a nice, squishy chair that even a rambunctious puppy cannot refuse.

The French Bulldogs on the following page were suited up with some sporty props for their portraits. The accessories helped to tell a story about the pups' personalities while adding visual interest in the frame.

These sporty props were selected to tell a story about each dog's playful personality.

Little Boy · CHAMP · Pre-Pre · Show Dog · Little Beowulf · CUTIE · Secretariat · Priam · Prius · Priam · A-HOLE · BIG BOY · Dick · King of Troy · BABE · Sweet Boy · Loner · Shorty · RICHARD · Priam · Jekyll & Hyde · BABY Nut · Little Dick · Priam · Cutie Pie · HANDSOME · Sweetie Pie · Sweetie · Mama's Boy

WHAT'S IN A NAME?

The idea for this portrait came about when I realized how many nicknames my husband and I had for our Boxer, Gromit. I had my dog's "What's in a Name?" portrait hanging on the wall when I met with my client, and she fell in love with it. We made one for her dog, Priam.

The outcome was fun and quirky. Do you know how many nicknames you have for your dog, cat, or horse? Start listing your pet's nicknames; you will be surprised.

BUDDHA

I can't get enough of French Bulldogs. I have gotten to know quite a few of them over the years, and I simply adore their snorty grunts, wiggly bodies, and the way they come charging at me for attention.

This little pea was so amazing! At just 2 months old, she came in to my studio for her debut portrait. She brought along her brothers and sisters too, but these portraits were all about her.

I can't get enough of French Bulldogs. I simply adore their snorty grunts, wiggly bodies, and the way they come charging at me for attention.

POISE AND A POUT

L et's face it: dogs can be very expressive. Take a look at the way Gatsby's demeanor changed during our winter-themed session. In the first image *(below)*, he is sitting pretty. He is looking at the camera and is perfectly poised. In the second image *(right),* he appears to have had his fill of having his picture taken. Gatsby was pouting, which his owner said he is notorious for when he doesn't get his way. The portrait that shows Gatsby pout-

Sometimes, outtakes can be a bigger hit than even the "perfect" photograph taken during the session.

ing is one of his peoples' favorite photos because they feel it accurately shows his real attitude.

Sometimes, outtakes can be a bigger hit than even the "perfect" photograph taken during the session.

RILEY

ere's Riley, a Cane Corso, at 9 months old. I wanted the focus of his images to be on his big, beautiful eyes. Riley is an amazingly well-behaved dog who weighs in around 100 pounds. He is a sight to see, too; he has a dark-brindle coat, captivating light eyes, and a striking, proud posture.

THE PERFECT SUBJECT

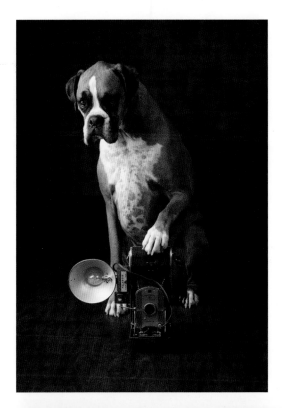

Boxers are funny. They believe they are lap dogs, so any lap is theirs. They think they are small, and they can curl up into the tiniest spaces.

This image of Gromit in a cream-colored chair is one of the last studio portraits taken of him. It was taken only 3 months before we knew he was ill and passed. He loved to hang out with me. As soon as I had everything set up and metered my lights, he would go hop up on which ever piece of furniture was available and nap.

Whether I was photographing him with an old camera, or piquing his curiosity by blowing bubbles, he was always the perfect subject.

section three

WORKING AND SERVICE DOGS

RICHARD AND PATRIOT

Richard was diagnosed with multiple sclerosis, a degenerative disease, when he was 32 years old, 27 years ago. Richard said he hadn't actually thought of a service dog; he had heard that there was only a 30 percent passing rate and that he was going to look into finding a "drop out" pup, one that didn't quite make the cut but had a great upbringing and some training. He didn't think he was the right candidate until someone suggested he actually look at getting a licensed service dog. He and his wife Jacqueline started gathering information and discovered Canine Companions for Independence (CCI), based in Santa Rosa. They took a tour of the facility and were impressed by what they learned and saw. The application process took 6 months, followed by interviews and waiting—lots and lots of waiting. There was a point when Richard said he thought they had forgotten about him and he had almost given up hope of receiving a service dog. After 2 years, he finally received notice he was accepted into the program.

The best and hardest part was yet to come. Richard and his wife were to stay on campus and train with dogs for a couple of weeks. The couple packed their bags and headed to CCI, along with 10 other recipients who would be training alongside them.

For the first few days, everyone there worked with all of the dogs, learning how to give the dogs specific commands; meanwhile the staff evaluated how each person worked with each dog and how each dog worked with each person.

On a Wednesday, all the dogs were lined up in their kennels. One by one the recipients were called to the center where blankets were laid out. Richard's name was called. He and Jacqueline headed to the blanket, sat down and waited. With so much excitement, so many overwhelming feelings, they announced Patriot. Her crate door was opened and she was brought over to them, and tears of joy were shed. They knew this would be the beginning of a long and wonderful relationship. All 11 recipients went through the same process.

Richard mentioned he had taken a liking to a different dog and asked why she was not the right dog for him. It was explained that because of his balance/stability issues, which would change over time, he required a dog who was stable and sure, and the dog he had hoped for was a bit skittish. Richard was amazed at how the trainers thought of everything and really did their homework on each person's needs and each dog's abilities.

Now for the hard work! The next week and a half would entail extensive training with their new dog, followed by a written test and a live test that would take place at a shopping mall.

The process seemed long and overwhelming at times, but oh so worth it as Patriot has become a huge part of their family.

section four

FUN IN THE SUN

SAND AND SURF

Dogs' personalities shine through during a visit to a sandy beach. Here, Remington *(above)* ran full-speed, and I was able to capture him with all four feet off the ground. His brother, AJ *(following page, top)*, sat perfectly while his hair blew in the wind. Kiley *(following page, bottom)* is a working dog—she was all business.

CHOCOLATE DOODLE

Meet Cooper, a 14-month-old Australian Labradoodle. Our day started at the Pelican Point Beach, which wraps around a rocky point toward Redondo Beach here in Half Moon Bay, CA. It turned out to be an absolutely beautiful day with blue skies.

OCEAN ANNIE

Annie is a Portuguese Water Spaniel, so setting her up for a portrait with the ocean in the background on a bright, sunny day seemed an ideal approach.

Photo tip: If you have a dark-haired dog like Annie and want to take a flattering outdoor photo of your pup in a favorite location, try positioning your dog so that the sun is in his or her face. This will help to get some light in the dog's eyes.

. . . try positioning your dog so that the sun is in his or her face. This will help to get some light in the dog's eyes.

IN BODIE

Gromit was my muse—the light of my life and the pain in my butt. He taught me more about dogs, dog behavior, and working with dogs than any book ever could. He was a superstar at modeling and was my studio mascot. Everyone who met Gromit loved him. He was a very proud and regal Boxer who would do almost anything I asked of him.

One of my favorite photos of Gromit was taken in Bodie, a ghost town in California. I had him sit on the porch of one of the old houses in the town. It seemed to me his expression had an outlaw feel that complements the location and tells a story.

Everyone who met Gromit loved him. He was a very proud and regal Boxer . . .

LAND SHARK

This old guy *(below)* loved to plop down on the sand and scoot. I photographed him from a low angle to create a larger-than-life feeling that is well suited to his big personality.

Watch, listen, and learn from the dogs around you. Each one has a distinctive personality and will do some strange and funny things.

COMET

This is Comet, an Australian Shepherd who, though he is a senior in dog years, is certainly young at heart. His eyes lit up when his owner and I took him to the beach for a photo session. The tide was low—which was a good thing, as Comet does not enjoy getting wet—and I was able to capture some beautiful storytelling portraits with soft, muted colors and subtle reflections.

Less than a block away, I photographed Comet by an old bridge covered in graffiti. The two juxtaposed image styles helped to show different sides of Comet's personality and also helped tell the story of his special day out on the town.

ON A GLOOMY DAY

This particular day was quite gray and gloomy—not the kind of day you would normally consider to be an ideal opportunity to head out to photograph at the beach. On this day, it seemed as if the sky would open up any minute, and it would start pouring.

I loved the texture in the sky and the sand during a low tide. I placed Gromit in a sit/stay position, a skill he learned during one of our many training sessions. At that moment, he turned to watch a few other dogs in the distance behind me. This allowed me to create a very nice portrait.

A split second after I captured the image, Gromit was off running and playing. It only takes one shot.

At that moment, he turned to watch a few other dogs in the distance behind me. This allowed me to create a very nice portrait.

ENZO

This trio of images of Enzo shows a few of his many moods. I love his crazy gaze, head tilt, and floppy ear in the first image *(previous page, top)*. In the second image *(previous page, bottom)*, I was able to capture him with his jowls flapping and teeth showing as he took off after a ball that was thrown just out of camera range.

The third image *(below)* shows Enzo's cute and cuddly side—and his boundless love for his dad.

Enzo is a real joy to be around. He is well-behaved and—when he's not hunting down a cherished toy—he tends to be calm, cool, and collected.

WATER DOGS

Photographing this pair of Duck Tolling Retreivers *(following page)* on a sunny day at the beach was a lot of fun. I had two goals for this location portrait session: to capture the distinct personality of each dog and to get a portrait of the pair that would depict their bond.

The male dog, named Bud *(below, top)*, is typically quiet and reserved. When his toy came out, though, he was intensely focused and driven to play.

Cali *(below, bottom)*, on the other hand, is incredibly intense by nature. During our session, she stalked her toy until her owner decided to throw it.

I had two goals for this location portrait session:

to capture the distinct personality of each dog and to get a

portrait of the pair that would depict their bond.

PACK MENTALITY

BEST FRIENDS

Aside from living under the same roof and sharing some distant French roots, Wallace and Isla are total opposites and an unlikely pair who became fast friends. Wallace, 130 pounds, who has been likened to Ferdinand the Bull, has no idea he is a massive, imposing Dogue de Bordeaux, with an intimidating voice. In fact, he has only barked a dozen or so times in his 7 years of life. He is content to sit in the grass and watch the world go by. Then there is Isla—Isla Bean or the Bean, as she is often called—is 2-year-old French Bulldog who weighs in at just 20 pounds. She is a whirlwind of energy and is always on the move. She constantly has a toy in her mouth and drops it only to chase bees and butterflies in the yard.

Watching these two interact was wonderful. Wallace did everything slowly and thoughtfully, and Isla would run headlong into any situation, often ignoring Wallace's pace and having to run under him to get where she was going faster. Playtime looked like something straight from Wrestlemania. Wallace would lie on his side while Isla stood on him and chewed on his ears, loose skin, or tail. With a gentle sweep of his paw or by sitting up, he could rid himself of Isla's needle teeth, but in a minute, she would go at him again.

After the roughhousing, a nap was needed. Wallace chose the spot and Isla found a curve to nestle into. They slept like that until it was time to do it all over again.

PUPS IN PROPS

To create the image of the German Shorthaired Pointers *(above)*, I photographed each of the six pups separately, then combined their images into one frame in postproduction. I call this image *Pantone Pups*. The image was accepted into the International Photographic Competition Loan Collection. It is one of the highest honors awarded by Professional Photographers of America.

The pups in cups *(above)* are a Pug/ Boston Terrier/Chihuahua mix. I photographed them when they were almost 7 weeks old. They are funny little pups with huge personalities. Their momma was very pregnant when she was rescued by an individual who had a long history of working with dogs. The woman kept her through her pregnancy and the birthing of the pups.

She fell in love with the momma and kept her and one of the darling little puppies too, then adopted the rest of the litter out.

My Dot is shown in the brown cup. This photo was taken about a month before I realized that she was to be our forever dog.

THE WHOLE LITTER

At just 8 weeks old, this litter of German Shorthaired Pointer pups was ready to take on the world! At this age, puppies are full on energy. It takes a lot to wear them out.

Photographing a single young puppy this age requires patience. When there are a group of rambunctious puppies, the challenges inherent in capturing a photo in which every dog looks his or her best is

amplified. Many times, photographers will photograph an individual dogs or dogs in smaller groups and then create a composite in postproduction. This was not the case here, however. A team of assistants placed the litter on the antique trunk and got their attention. I worked quickly to get the shot.

Puppies are not too keen on staying where they are positioned. This crew kept leaping off of the trunk, so I had a thick rug, folded in half, placed in front of the them to provide a little cushion and traction for them when they made the daring leap.

TWO SISTERS

These fluffy Saint Bernard pups were just over 8 weeks old when they were brought to my studio for photographs. Their owner wanted a portrait with a clean, contemporary look, so I positioned the pups in a mid-century modern shell chair *(following page)* to help contain them and give the portrait some flair.

Puppies grow so quickly. I wanted to photograph these two using a prop *(below)* that would serve as a good indicator of their relatively tiny size at this point in their lives. As adults, Saint Bernards may weigh between 110 and 240 pounds!

As adults, Saint Bernards may weigh between 110 and 240 pounds!

FAMILY

Documenting the love a human has for her four-legged family members is an important goal for pet photographers. My client wanted to put her love for her dogs (and her boots!) on display—so I photographed a series of shots in my studio to provide lots of photo options for her walls. As you can see, the woman truly puts her pups on a pedestal.

INDEX

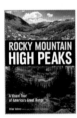

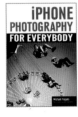

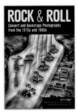

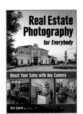